*A PORTFOLIO OF EARLY ULSTER PHOTOGRAPHY*

Shadows on Glass

*BRIAN MERCER WALKER*

The Appletree Press Ltd

*Dedicated to my Aunts Issy, Berta and Jessena,*
*and to my Uncle Thomas Walker*

Published by
The Appletree Press Ltd
19-21 Alfred Street
Belfast BT2 8DL

Published with assistance
of The Arts Council of Northern Ireland

A catalogue record for this book is
available from the British Library

ISBN 0 86281 311 5

This impression 1994

# CONTENTS

# INTRODUCTION

In compiling this book on early Ulster photography, I have not been concerned with tracing in detail the technical development of photography in Ulster but have sought to illustrate social life in the province between the late 1860's and approximately 1920 through the work and lives of a number of early photographers. Each chapter has been devoted to a different photographer dealing with a special subject or theme. Some of these photographers were people of importance in photographic or other fields but most were unknown outside their own immediate circles. All of them are of special importance to us, however, because they have left us unique records of their lives and times.

News of the startling success of Louis Daguerre and Fox Talbot in early 1839 in obtaining permanent photographic images had been greeted with much interest in Ulster as elsewhere. On 19 February 1839, the *Belfast Newsletter* carried a lengthy account of Daguerre's work, referring to it as a 'singular and interesting discovery'. A year and a half later, on 6 August, 1840, the *Northern Whig* reported that a local engraver, F.S. Beatty, had made a photogenic drawing of the Long Bridge in Belfast; Beatty later claimed to have conducted photographic experiments for several years prior to this. In October 1842 an advertisement appeared in the local press announcing that a Daguerrotype company had commenced to take portraits at No.20, Castle Street, Belfast. By 1861 there were 19 professional photographers in Ulster; twenty years later there were 83 and by 1901 the number had risen to 234. The number of amateur photographers also increased, and in 1885 the Ulster Amateur Photographic Society was founded.

It is sometimes difficult today to appreciate the enthusiasm with which the discovery and early development of photography was greeted. In 1864, John Rorke, a former master at Dungannon Royal School, wrote a poem, nearly 4,000 lines long, called *Fancies on the photograph* (Dublin), in which he praised photography and recalled what it had brought to modern man. Thanks to photography, he pointed out, it was possible to obtain portraits that were more lifelike than paintings: beautiful buildings and famous people could be easily recorded and displayed: old friends and familiar scenes could be pictured accurately for later viewing. Besides all this, Rorke stated, photography provided an important, new form of historical record.

The life which our photographers viewed through their cameras was very different from today. Society in Ulster was mainly rural: in 1871, 18 per cent of the population lived in towns of 2,000 or more, while in 1911 the figure was 38 per cent. The countryside contained a wide array of social groups. These ranged from the gentry, whose life style we can observe through the private, family photographs of Mary Alice Young, to the labourers and smallholders, who were recorded so vividly in Rose Shaw's work. Country towns, with their quiet streets, uncluttered, except on market day, were very different from the towns of the present. The photographs of J.W. Burrows of Strabane well illustrate life in a typical country town, before and during the advent of the motor car.

By 1911 the population of Belfast had grown to nearly 400,000 compared with 174,000 in 1871. The work of an unknown photographer of the early 1870's, shows the main streets and building of the prosperous, expanding Belfast. Another side of this growth, however, can be seen in the stark photographs of Belfast slums in 1911. These and other aspects of the varied and changing ways of life in Ulster in the period have been recorded through the lens of our photographers. The book is primarily a social history and no attempt has been made to deal with political events which in any case were not widely recorded, due to the limited capabilities of the contemporary camera.

Most of the photographs included here are published for the first time. Some are from well known collections but others are from collections which have only come to light in the last few years, having been locked away after the photographers' deaths. Brief moments of light and shade captured by the photographer on fragile, plate glass negatives, these photographs present us today with lasting and strong images of a lost world. In John Rorke's glowing words,

> *Once poets sang — and could not sing more —*
> *'Events advancing cast their shades before —'*
> *But now departing forms leave shades behind,*
> *And all you loved is spared to eye and mind.*
> *Be grateful then for such celestial aid;*
> *Time was man could not rescue even a shade.*

*Brian M. Walker* 7

# Mary Alice Young

Mary Alice Young was the eldest daughter of the Rt Hon. Sir F.E.W. Macnaghten, bt. When she was born in 1867 the family owned nearly 8000 acres at Bushmills, Co. Antrim. In 1893 she married W.R. Young, eldest son of the Rt Hon. John Young, owner of Galgorm castle and an estate of almost 2000 acres, near Ballymena, Co. Antrim. Four years later, she and her husband went to live at Galgorm. When the Rt Hon. John Young died in 1915, her husband succeeded to the castle and estate. In her background and interests Mary Young was like many another daughter of the gentry but unlike most she was also an enthusiastic and accomplished photographer.

Between 1890 and 1915 she took over a thousand photographs, often experimenting with light and composition in her work. Nearly all these were concerned with her family and life on the Galgorm estate. The subjects included family groups, the estate workers, the castle and grounds and friends and relatives enjoying themselves at croquet, tennis, fishing or other popular pastimes of the period. Her photographs provide a valuable personal insight into the life-style of the gentry in the decades prior to the first world war.

When Mary Young was born the gentry played a dominant role in Ulster society. They owned most of the land which they let to tenant farmers. As a rule they were magistrates, members of grand juries and poor law boards of guardians, which looked after local government affairs, and they often presided over local societies and associations. But, due to growing tensions between landlords and tenants in the 1870's and the bad harvests of 1879 and 1880, with the consequent growth of the Land League and tenant right associations, the dominance of the landlords was weakened. The 1881 land act gave the tenants important new rights over their holdings and the Ashbourne act of 1885 began a process of land purchase which, by the first world war, had resulted in most of the tenants obtaining the ownership of their farms. In addition the local government act of 1898 set up county councils which diffused control of local government over a wider spectrum of society. However, the gentry still remained quite influential in the countryside.

The Youngs had in fact been prosperous merchants in Ballymena in the early nineteenth century and had bought Galgorm only in 1850 from the earl of Mountcashel. But clearly they had no difficulty in integrating into gentry circles. Mary's father-in-law was a privy councillor, a deputy lieutenant and a justice of the peace. The family was on good terms with many of the other landed families in Co. Antrim and there was much coming and going between Galgorm and other county houses, especially among the younger people for parties and outings.

Most of the Youngs' land was sold to the tenants under the terms of the 1903 Wyndham act, but the family retained the castle and about 300 acres of gardens, woods and farmland. The reduction of the estate did not have much immediate effect on life in the castle. Until the first world war there were never fewer than 6 domestic servants, and labourers, coachmen, gardeners and gamekeepers on the estate usually numbered around 15. A governess came daily from Belfast to teach the Youngs' only child, Hilda Grace, born in 1896.

For Mary Young, life at Galgorm must have been quite busy. Her husband's step-mother had died shortly before she and her husband moved to the castle and she took over supervision of the household. Besides her husband, daughter and father-in-law, her husband's 5 brothers and 7 sisters frequently stayed at the castle. When the war came she busied herself organising comforts for the troops and it seems to have been this which caused her to give up her photography, through lack of spare time. She died in 1946.

Mary Young at Dundarave, Bushmills, her parents' home, on her wedding day, 28 Aug. 1893.

9

A family group at Galgorm, 1900. Those standing are, from left to right: William, the photographer's husband; George, a brother-in-law; Janet, a sister-in-law; and Ogilvie Blair-Graham, husband of Grace, a sister-in-law. Those seated are, from left to right: Mrs Grace Blair-Graham; Ogilvie Blair-Graham, a nephew; Rt Hon. John Young, her father-in-law; Hilda, her daughter; and a friend. Like many of the gentry, John Young was a justice of the peace, a deputy lieutenant and also a privy councillor.

Left: Galgorm castle from the front gate, c.1900. The castle was in the centre of a fortified bawn; both bawn and castle were built in the seventeenth century. In the 1830's large sash windows were inserted in the castle to allow more light in the interior. Flemish style curves were added to the battlements and to the doorcase, and a new sloped roof was constructed. In the 1850's the front drive was built, walled gardens were laid out and trees planted around the castle. The bawn walls were repaired under the supervision of the Belfast architect, Sir Charles Lanyon. The wall at the front was only partly repaired, perhaps in order to create a 'romantic ruin' effect.

Hilda, Mary Young's daughter, busily at work on her embroidery in the nursery, 1907. The sewing basket was a Christmas gift from the family grocer in Galgorm village. Also, Hilda and a friend reading a magazine. The romantic charm of the pictures shows the photographer's skill in the use of light.

George and Janet Young playing croquet
c.1895. The origins of croquet lie in medieval
times but the sport became popular only in the
middle of the nineteenth century when it
became fashionable at county house parties: by
1900, however, it had been overtaken in
popularity by tennis.

Mary Young aboard a phaeton coach at her parents' home at Dundarave, c.1894.
Below: Patrick, another brother-in-law, c.1910. Horse riding and hunting were favourite sports of the Irish gentry.

Skating—with precautions!

Hilda, the photographer's sister, with her watercolours in a cornfield, c.1900. Watercolouring and embroidery were favourite pastimes among young women from a well-to-do background.

Right: Soldiers of the North Irish Horse watering their mounts near the parish church in Antrim, 1915. This was one of the last photographs taken by Mary Young. Both of her brothers were army officers, as were several cousins and brothers-in-law.

# William Fee McKinney

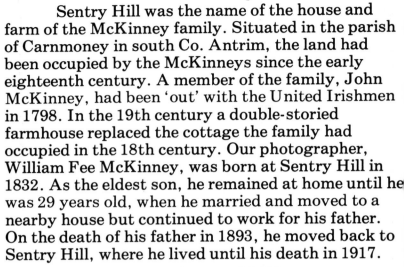

Sentry Hill was the name of the house and farm of the McKinney family. Situated in the parish of Carnmoney in south Co. Antrim, the land had been occupied by the McKinneys since the early eighteenth century. A member of the family, John McKinney, had been 'out' with the United Irishmen in 1798. In the 19th century a double-storied farmhouse replaced the cottage the family had occupied in the 18th century. Our photographer, William Fee McKinney, was born at Sentry Hill in 1832. As the eldest son, he remained at home until he was 29 years old, when he married and moved to a nearby house but continued to work for his father. On the death of his father in 1893, he moved back to Sentry Hill, where he lived until his death in 1917.

Besides being a farmer, McKinney was a man of many interests with an absorbing love of the countryside. He built up a fine collection of fossils,

stoneaxes and minerals from the surrounding district, for which he built a special room at Sentry Hill. He collected ballads and books of local poetry and compiled family histories of the Carnmoney people up to the late nineteenth century. The Linenhall Library, Belfast, made him an honorary member for his many donations of rare books. A keen member of the Belfast Naturalist Field Club, McKinney was also a relative and close friend of F.J. Bigger, the well known Ulster antiquarian and historian. In 1869 he helped to found the Carnmoney Mutual Improvement Society, a local debating and literary society.

This intense interest in his own locality was carried into his hobby of photography which he took up in the 1880's. He photographed not only his family and friends but also everyday life on the farm: the men who worked in the fields and the many craftsmen and artisans who visited the farm, such as the journeyman tailor, the carpenter and the butcher. The small farmers and their families in the area too, received the attention of his camera. Altogether 600 plates were carefully labelled and stored. His work is a fascinating study of life in this one small rural community.

The McKinney farm was a very substantial and prosperous one and the McKinneys were regarded as gentlemen farmers. Unlike most nineteenth century farms which, prior to the land purchase acts, were held on yearly tenancies, the farm at Sentry Hill was held on a perpetuity lease obtained in the 1830's from the landowners, the Donegall family, who were then in bad financial straits. When William Fee McKinney took over the farm in 1893 it consisted of 70 acres at Sentry Hill and another 30 acres nearby. Normally there were 3 full time labourers on the farm while in the house there was a maid and a daily charwoman. At seed and harvest time small farmers in the district were employed to do the extra work.

Left: W.F. McKinney in the conservatory of Sentry Hill, c.1900.

A summer's afternoon in the garden at Sentry
Hill, 1898. McKinney's daughter, Meg, is
**22** pouring the tea for 2 friends.

Family and friends at Sentry Hill 1900. They are, from left to right: Rev. Hugh Waterworth, local presbyterian minister; Miss Bird a friend; Fergus Wilson, manager of the Blackstaff Mills, Belfast; John McKinney (standing), the photographer's son; Tom McKinney, his grandson; Miss Chisolm, Leigan Field, Carnmoney; W.H. Boyd, Carntall, Carnmoney; and Elsie McKinney, his grandaughter. As the eldest son, John McKinney remained at home to look after the farm, which he eventually inherited. Tom, his only son, aged 6 in this photograph, died on 19 July, 1916, from wounds received at the battle of the Somme.

Left: Sam Williamson, thatcher, c.1895.

Below Right: Tom Couley, pig killer, c.1895. Couley travelled from farm to farm slaughtering pigs for the farmers' own use.

Below: Alex McIlwaine at work with a team of plough horses while young Tom McKinney, the photographer's grandson, looks on, 1907. In accord with general custom, McIlwaine, as ploughman, was the leading farm hand at Sentry Hill. He was employed there for over 60 years.

Below: Erecting a specially designed corrugated iron hay shed on the farm, Sept. 1903 — one of the first in the district. The job was carried out by the Belfast firm, Potts and Houston. Substantial farmers like McKinney were to the fore in introducing new farming techniques and employing the latest machinery and materials.

Left: Joshua Wells, journeyman tailor, c.1890. He visited farms, staying for periods of up to 2 weeks, making suits for the men folk. He is pictured here at work, sitting on the kitchen table.

Above: Sam Black, handyman, c.1890.

Below: Tom Montgomery, carpenter, c.1890.

The Guthrie brothers, small farmers, at King's Moss, near Sentry Hill, c.1895: from left to right, Sam (1805-1901), John (1805-1902) and James (1822-1901). They were relatives of the photographer.

The McClenaghan family at their home in Ballycraigy, c.1890. Small farmers like the McClenaghans assisted the McKinneys at busy times of the year, sometimes for pay and sometimes in return for the use of the McKinneys' horses and machines.

Left: William Macartney and his daughters at Ballycraigy, near Sentry Hill, 1898. When this photograph was taken Macartney was 100 years old. He was born in the year of the '98 rebellion and was already middle-aged by the time of the famine.

# William Alfred Green

For the best record of the life and agricultural practice of the Ulster small farmer of over 50 years ago, we must turn to the work of a photographer, William Alfred Green (1870-1958), whose early working years were spent, not in the country but in commerce in Belfast. Born in Co. Down, Green entered the firm of a great uncle, Forster Green, a prominent Belfast tea merchant. However, poor health obliged him to give up this career and in order to work outdoors as much as possible he took up photography. He served his time with R.J. Welch, the leading contemporary Ulster photographer, and then went into business on his own, around 1910.

Green lived and worked at first in Belfast and afterwards in Antrim town. His photographs covered a wide range of subjects, and were in great demand for book illustrations, postcards, advertisements and educational lantern slides. They included much topographical material and many botanical and geological pictures. But Green's significance as a photographer lies not so much in these fields as in his brilliant studies of agricultural practices and folk custom. This was a subject that no other contemporary photographer in Ireland studied in such depth.

Many of his agricultural photographs were taken in the Toome area of mid-Co. Antrim. A relative of Green's lived there and through him he had an entrée into the local farming community, something that would normally have been difficult for a stranger. Green recorded the daily routine of the small farmers of 5-30 acres over the changing seasons. The photographs selected here are mostly from this Toome area. Their exact dates are not known but all were taken between 1910 and 1930. Although some may be later than the majority of photographs in the book, they show agricultural practices which had changed little from the previous 50 years.

Most of the farmers in Ulster, both large and

small, went in for mixed farming. The principal crops were oats, potatoes and flax. However, the most important part of the agricultural economy was livestock; in particular cattle, but also sheep, pigs and poultry. From the 1860's the proportion of land used for tillage declined steadily although during the first world war the decline was stopped for a brief period. There were, of course, differences in the types of farming followed on the various sizes of holdings. On the smaller farms a higher proportion of land was devoted to crops and of the cattle kept, a higher proportion was raised for dairy purposes, than on the larger farms.

The small farmers, photographed by Green, were the largest section of the farming community in Ulster. In 1911, of the 188,424 occupiers of land in the province, 3.1 per cent had 100 acres or more, 7.9 per cent 50-100 acres, 12.9 per cent 30-50 acres, 55.2 per cent 5-30 acres and 20.9 per cent under 5 acres. Farms were generally much smaller than in Great Britain and there were fewer agricultural labourers in the rural population: most of the work on the land was performed by the farmers and members of their families, although there were usually labourers on the larger farms.

However, the number of farms below 30 acres and especially below 15 acres was falling, because they were economically unviable, while the number of farms above 30 acres was increasing, a trend that had been going on since the famine. In addition, with the decline of domestic industries in the countryside in the second half of the nineteenth century and with fewer opportunities of casual labour, the families of small farmers were often obliged to leave home. The resulting drop in the rural population was not peculiar to Ulster but since there was little opportunity for other employment, except to a limited extent in Belfast, the only alternative for many was emigration.

In most parts of the country turf was the principal fuel. After being cut from a bog the turf was allowed to dry. It was then carefully stacked, as seen in this photograph, in order to keep it dry during the winter.

Removing flax from a lint hole. After it had been grown and pulled flax was retted (rotted) in these small, specially constructed ponds. The retting caused the outside of the stem to rot and the fibres to separate. The process produced a very unpleasant smell but flax was a good cash crop, especially for the small farmer. However, by the beginning of the twentieth century strong competition from flax growers in other countries like Belgium and Russia had caused a severe reduction in the acreage under flax.

This woman is using a plunge churn to make butter. The churning caused the butter fat to float to the top. The butter was then skimmed from the churn, washed and salted to make it keep. The buttermilk left in the churn was used for baking. The growth of co-operative creameries in the late nineteenth and early twentieth centuries ended most of this home churning except for personal use.

Working a corn fiddle to sow seed. The sower is carefully measuring his step in order to ensure a regular distribution of the seed. His young helper is following with a further supply.

Dairying, which required a lot of work, was most common on the smaller farms where the farmer's family provided the labour. Calves were usually sold to the larger farms for fattening.

Harvest time in the cornfield. On occasions such as this all the family, assisted by the neighbours, helped in the fields. The women are gathering the corn after it has been cut by the reaper. The sheaves of corn are being stooked by the man in the foreground to allow them to dry. A field of completed stooks can be seen in the middle distance.

Overleaf: When the harvest was over all who had helped gathered in the farmer's home for a celebration meal known as the 'harvest home'. The last sheaf of the harvest was usually hung over the table.

# Henry Tommasco Hutton

For all members of the farming community market and fair days were of great importance. Markets were held weekly in most towns and villages for the sale of general produce and fairs were held less frequently for the sale of livestock and the hiring of labour. They provided for the assembly and sorting of goods, for legalised transactions, for helping farmers to get a competitive price for their products and giving them an opportunity to purchase necessary implements and other requirements. They were also of course great social occasions.

One such market for which good photographic records have survived, was held in Ballynahinch, Co. Down, a town with a population of one and a half thousand in 1891. A few years earlier C.H. Bassett in his *County Down guide and directory* (Dublin, 1886), described the town and its market in the following manner:

*"Ballynahinch consists of a square and several streets . . . Being situated in the centre of a first-rate agricultural country, . . . the market for farm produce, held every Thursday, is stocked to repletion, and buyers are numerous. There is no town in the county where the market produces so complete a transformation from the routine of daily life. Every street has its scene of bustling activity, and in the Market Square, at some time of the day, all the energy is concentrated."*

A large variety of produce was sold at Ballynahinch market, including pork, grain, hay, potatoes, butter, eggs, fowl and flour. Some streets were specially reserved for certain produce while general goods were sold in the market square.

By the early decades of the twentieth century, however, local markets were a much less important part of the rural economy. The growth of co-operative creameries which sold butter direct to merchants resulted in the virtual disappearance of this product from the markets. The advent of motor transport encouraged the sale of produce on farms, and the setting up of marketing boards in the 1920's to regulate prices and the sale of certain products such as pork and eggs, dealt the local markets a hard blow. For many small towns like Ballynahinch the decline of the market had a detrimental effect on their prosperity.

The photographer who recorded market day in Ballynahinch in its hey-day in the 1890's was Henry Tommasco Hutton (1874-1952). From a well-to-do background, he spent most of his life in Donaghadee, Co. Down. A man of many parts, he was not only an able photographer but also a successful inventor, and was responsible for devising an early foot pump for pneumatic car tyres. However, he lost most of his money through a collapse in Irish railway shares in which he had invested heavily. Hutton then turned to work full-time at another interest of his, market gardening. This interest perhaps explains the Ballynahinch market photographs.

In holding a weekly market Ballynahinch was typical of many Ulster towns but it was unique in having, only 2 miles from the town, a well known spa, something which Hutton also recorded with his camera. The spa consisted of several springs of sulphure-chalybeate water which, it was popularly believed, helped general health and also assisted people with scrofulous diseases. There was a hotel in the area for visitors and other accommodation was available in local farmhouses. The grounds at the spa were pleasantly laid out and included a famous labyrinth. Advertisements for the hotel described the spa as the 'Wiesbaden of the north', but after a brief period of popularity in the late nineteenth century it declined as a holiday attraction.

Above right: The photographer H.T. Hutton.

Right: A peaceful scene in the grove at the spa, Ballynahinch, c.1895.

Church Street in Ballynahinch on market day with a wide variety of farmers' carts in the foreground, c.1895.

Left: Dromore Street, where cereals were brought and sold, c.1895.

Right: 'Any buyers, any buyers' — salesman in Market Square, c.1895

Below left: Market Square, in the centre of the town, with crowds listening to the salesmen and stallholders, c.1895.

Below right: Ballynahinch station, c.1895. The development of the railways in Co. Down in the second half of the nineteenth century brought increased trade to Ballynahinch market as it gave access to outlying districts and allowed easier passage of produce to Belfast.

Market Square, with furniture and animal troughs for sale, as well as clothes and general goods, c.1895.

Lettie Hutton, the photographer's sister, and Elsie McMinn, a cousin, on their bicycles at the spa near one of the spa pump huts.

Below right: An interior of one of the huts with an attendant at the pump. David Ker, whose name is inscribed on the pump label, was the former landlord of Ballynahinch and the Spa. He erected the pumps and sought to develop the area.

# John S. Holden

John Sinclair Holden (1837-1923) was a medical doctor with a great interest in archaeology, photography and geology. After qualifying at Queen's College, Belfast, in 1865, Holden practised for a time at Glenarm, Co. Antrim, and then went to Sudburn in southern England where he spent the remainder of his life. A founder member of the Belfast Naturalist Field Club, he took a considerable number of photographs between 1867 and 1870, showing the antiquities, geology, houses and harbours of the east Antrim coast. His interest in geology led him to deliver an address to the field club in 1868 on the Co. Antrim iron ore deposts, urging that they be fully exploited to bring prosperity and employment to the country.

How influential this address was in arousing interest in the Antrim iron deposits it is difficult to say, but we may note that mining of the deposits grew rapidly in the following years. The existence of the ore had been known for some time but serious mining had begun only in the early 1860's. In 1862 just over 10,000 tons were exported and by 1870 the figure had trebelled. The next decade saw an even more dramatic rise in production of the ore and in 1880 a high point was reached with the export of 230,000 tons. However, while the deposits were enormous, the ore was not of a high quality and there were increasing difficulties in mining it. By the early 1900's output had fallen to around 100,000 tons and by 1924 work in the mines had stopped altogether, although it was revived for a short time during the second world war.

The harbours of Carnlough and Red Bay, photographed by Holden, were used to export much of the iron ore. Red Bay harbour, near Cushendall and Waterfoot, dealt with the traffic from the Glenravel mines, and an aerial ropeway was built in the early 1870's to carry the ore from the mines to Red Bay. Another important cargo carried from Red Bay was limestone. During the 1860's and 1870's these east Antrim harbours were improved and for a time they prospered but the subsequent development of roads and railways in the region removed much of their trade.

Up until the middle of the nineteenth century small wooden vessels dominated the shipping world. In the latter half of the century, with the expansion of trade and the development of shipbuilding techniques, new, larger ships were constructed with metal and steam gradually replacing wood and sails. But for the carrying of cargoes to and from minor ports, small sailing ships such as schooners and ketches maintained their importance. These ships continued to carry cargoes, especially raw materials like iron, granite and coal, around the Ulster coast and farther afield.

Many of the Ulster coastal schooners were owned by local merchants and were often built in local shipyards. The average schooner was manned by 3 men and a boy. Work was strenuous due to the hard labour in loading cargoes, pumping, and moving the heavy sails but payment was based on a share system of the profits. Two areas on the Ulster coast well known for their sailing tradition were Island Magee in Co. Antrim and the Mourne coastal region in Co. Down. The northern coastal sailing ships enjoyed a good trade in the second part of the nineteenth century but the drop off in demand for the raw materials from the local ports and the development of other transport facilities, both on land and sea, led to their virtual disappearance by the 1920's.

A small pleasure boat
belonging to the photographer.

Red Bay harbour, c.1870. The small one-masted ship in the foregound is a smack; the three-masted topsail ship on the right and the 2 double masted ships by the pier are schooners. These vessels were involved in trading around the coast and across the Irish sea but the schooners sometimes went to the Mediterranean and farther afield. Limestone was the principal cargo shipped from Red Bay in the early 1860's but by the early 1870's iron ore was being exported in large quantities.

Red Bay, c.1870. A smack and double masted schooner are lying on the beach. With their full bodied hulls these ships could sail into shallow coastal areas, beach and load their cargoes at low tide. Smacks were fairly rare by this time, having been replaced by slightly larger ships like ketches. These coastal sailing vessels were in common use up to the first world war, especially in areas where access by other means was difficult.

# Rose Shaw

Rose Shaw witnessed life in the Ulster countryside in the early decades of the twentieth century at both ends of the social scale. She was governess to the Gledstanes who lived at Fardross house, near Clogher, Co. Tyrone. She seems to have been regarded as part of the family and after her charges had grown up she returned annually to the house for a month's holiday in the summer. But, besides being attached to the Gledstane family, Rose Shaw had a great interest and admiration for the labourers and small farmers of the surrounding Clogher Valley, spending much of her time recording their folklore and photographing their way of life.

Between about 1905 and the early 1920's she took many photographs, developing them at Fardross in a windowless room off the dining room that was normally used for storing silver. Unfortunately only about 30 of her photographs seem to have survived. In 1930 she wrote *Carleton's country* (Dublin) with an introduction by Sir Shane Leslie. The book, which looked at the countryside and people of the Clogher Valley, where William Carleton had spent his early days, included a number of her photographs. What happened to Rose Shaw after 1930 or indeed where she originally came from is not known but she is still remembered affectionately by older people around Clogher. She succeeded in being accepted by the people she photographed, perhaps partly because they admired her intrepid spirit as she trekked around the countryside with her heavy camera.

These farmers and labourers amongst whom Rose Shaw moved were the poorest section in the countryside. The farmers were smallholders with only a few acres of land and some rough mountain grazing. With domestic industries disappearing and the need for casual labour declining due to increased mechanisation and the change from tillage to pasture, many emigrated because they had little opportunity to supplement their meagre incomes. Another factor in their numerical decline was that people came

Rose Shaw's photographs, such as this one of a young girl in her bare feet, have tremendous charm and beauty, while not concealing the poverty and harshness of the lives of these Clogher Valley women.

increasingly to expect a better living than could be made from such small farms.

In addition to casual labourers there were in the countryside full time unmarried labourers who stayed at their employers' farmhouses, and full time married labourers, who lived in tied cottages, with perhaps a few acres. Hiring fairs were held regularly and labourers were engaged by farmers for about 6 months at a time. Wages for labourers improved in the later nineteenth century but their lives remained very harsh and their numbers declined.

Moving around these small farmers' and labourers' homes, Rose Shaw photographed the women in particular. Besides doing household chores, the women helped with potato planting, turf-cutting and haymaking. The heavier work on the farm, such as ploughing and mowing, was carried out by the men, while the women were specially responsible for churning the milk and looking after the poultry.

Woman with wicker basket and dog in a country loanin (lane to cottage). She is probably going to collect eggs, an important source of income for the womenfolk.

Woman and child by the fire in a cottage. Above the woman's head can be seen a harnen stand for hardening oat cake in front of the fire. while a pot hangs over the fire from a chain. The floor is earthen

Right: This girl with a creel for collecting turf is wearing the typical dress of a country labouring woman — shawl, apron and skirt.

Right: Goats were frequently owned by small holders because they were good milk producers and would eat almost anything.

The young woman is spinning wool while her older companion is holding a ball of spun wool. The spinning wheel is an early type that was turned by hand. By this time it had been replaced nearly everywhere by the pedal operated Dutch spinning wheel.

At work in the oatfield gathering sheaves of oats. Even the children have been brought to this important event. This photograph shows the hilly nature of much of the land in the Clogher region.

# James Glass

The leading photographer in the north west of the province in the late nineteenth and early twentieth centuries was James Glass. Born in 1847, he established a business as a portrait and landscape photographer in Derry city in 1870 and by the 1890's he had several flourishing studios in the city. His success seems to have resulted from his portrait work. Glass offered to the public not only portraits in the form of ordinary photographs but also photographic pictures finished in crayon, oil and watercolour: a speciality of his was portraits executed on porcelain. He died in 1931.

However, while portraiture was Glass's main field and the one for which he was best known by contemporaries, it is for an album of extraordinary landscape photographs that he is remembered today. This album consists of 24 photographs which he took in the Gweedore district of the west Donegal highlands, apparently in the early 1870's. It is a unique record of life in the poorest part of the province and illustrates traditional methods of farming and living conditions that had already disappeared in most other places.

The area which Glass photographed was on the western sea-board and consisted of a wild mountainous region with quite densely populated lowlands along the coast. Even the best land in the coastal regions was infertile and the people eked a meagre living from raising cattle, sheep and hens, and growing potatoes, which were the main part of their diet. Seaweed was gathered for food and for sale as kelp to Scottish chemists. In the main they made their own clothes. There was little or no manufacturing industry except for the production of stockings, which the women undertook in their own homes. For seasonal work, children, from the age of 10 and upwards, frequently went to the Laggan district in south east Donegal while the older inhabitants went to Scotland. A bad season could bring severe distress to the area. Two decades later this

Glass's main studio in Derry, suitably decorated for the royal visit in 1903.

art of Donegal was placed under the auspices of the Congested Districts Board
hich was set up in 1891 to improve conditions in the poorest regions of the
ountry.

     In spite of opposition from the local landlord, some of the land was still
rmed on the rundale system, a method of farming that had once been widespread
Ireland. Under this system, land was jointly held by several families who
ivided it into long narrow strips, not contiguous with each other, a number of
hich were cultivated by each family. By the 1870's the system of rundale farming
ad disappeared from most of Ulster because it was inefficient, and was replaced
ith dispersed farms. The Gweedore district was one of the very few parts where it
rvived.

A stone and turf cabin
built into a hillside. The roof
consists of layers of turf sods and
gorse. The door is made out of a
bundle of hay attached to some
boards.

Cabins like this had no chimneys
and the smoke simply came out of
the doorway. Fortunately fuel in
the form of turf was plentiful,
which helped to make life in  this
windswept environment bearable.

Above left and right: Typical west Donegal longhouses which housed both people and animals. There was normally only one window, at the end near the fire where the family lived. The livestock were kept at the other end, on the downward slope if possible for drainage purposes. The projection at the back of the house above is a 'bed-outshot', which provided extra room for sleeping accommodation.

Left: This is probably a family group outside their home. Furniture in these houses usually consisted of a kitchen dresser, some chairs and beds of straw. Families of a dozen living in a cottage like this one were not uncommon. A piggin, which was used for keeping milk, can be seen lying on the ground on the left. As was the custom, the little boys are in skirts. This photograph shows how the thatch was firmly secured by cord tied to stone pegs in order to protect the roof against the high winds that were common in this area.

Most of these men are wearing traditional waistcoats, sometimes with cotton sleeves attached. The unusual waistcoat worn by the man standing third on the right, and some of the strange hats, may have been brought back to Gweedore by men working in Scotland. They may also have been charity hand-outs. During bad seasons the people in this area faced grave destitution and were often the object of charity from bodies like the London Irish Peasantry Society. The women's skirts were made from drugget, a coarse woollen fabric.

There were very few carts in the district. Goods were usually carried by horse or donkey or in creels on people's backs.

Right and below: These 2 photographs illustrate aspects of the rundale system of farming under which land was held in common by a number of families who lived in clusters of houses known as clachans. On the right can be seen 2 people working in the arable 'infield', which surrounded the clachan and which was separated by a wall from the 'outfield' where animals wandered freely: the 'infield' was divided into narrow strips for cultivation. Below is a photograph of a clachan. The arrangement of houses in the clachans was not as haphazard as it might appear. It was usually well planned so as to make the houses less open to the wind. The gables of the houses were rounded at the top and the thatch was made close to the gable wall, for purposes of wind resistance.

# J W Burrows

Strabane was a typical, prosperous, country town in early twentieth-century Ulster. With a population of 5107 in 1911 it was the second largest town in Co. Tyrone and one of 14 in the province with a population of over 5000. Situated on the river Mourne, it lay on the main railway line from Derry to Dublin and was also connected by narrow gauge railway to Killybegs and Letterkenny in nearby Co. Donegal. A canal ran from Strabane to the Foyle, thus linking the town by water to the port in Derry, and good roads radiated from the town to neighbouring areas. Like other large country towns, Strabane acted as an important commercial centre for the surrounding district. It provided employment in its shops and factories, carried out various local administrative tasks and provided social and other facilities for its inhabitants and visitors.

Fairs were held monthly and markets weekly on different days for various goods: the pork and grain markets were especially important. Strabane was a prosperous wholesaling and retailing centre and there were a number of large merchants' warehouses as well as shops dealing in a very wide variety of goods. There were also banks, insurance brokers, solicitors and auctioneers, and the town boasted a steam laundry and steam bakery. There were several shirt-making and underclothing factories and three miles outside the town at Sion Mills there were extensive flax mills.

As a local administrative centre Strabane had a main post-office, an R.I.C. barracks, a dispensary, a fever hospital, and a workhouse. Civic affairs were looked after by an urban district council elected by ratepayers. By the beginning of the century the main streets were paved, and sewerage, lighting and water were provided for the inhabitants. A new gas works was erected in the early 1900's at a cost of £20,000. There was a technical college in addition to several national and intermediate schools.

# STRABANE TOWN

There were 4 places of worship in the town - Church of Ireland, presbyterian, catholic and methodist. Social activity emanated from the lodges of the Orange Order and the Ancient Order of Hibernians, various men's social and recreational clubs, sports teams and bands. Other recreational facilities were offered by the Pallidrome theatre and cinema, and a dancehall. Touring dramatic societies visited the town. There were 2 newspapers, the *Strabane Chronicle* and the *Strabane Weekly News*.

By the early twentieth century no country town in Ulster was, of course, complete without its own photographer. From 1901 to 1913 this important service was provided by J.W. Burrows. His work involved taking studio portraits and also photographs at town events, sports days and important occasions; the latter were exhibited in his shop window so as to sell copies to those in the photographs. Besides being the town photographer Burrows opened and ran the Pallidrome and the local dancehall.

In 1913 he sold his business to H.F.T. Cooper, a Londoner, who settled in Strabane and was the town photographer until his death in 1960. The collection of Burrows and Cooper photographs numbers over 200,000 plate-glass negatives and is probably the largest single, commercial collection in Ireland. All the photographs in this chapter are the work of J.W. Burrows and so date between 1901 and 1913.

Left: Main Street, Strabane, c.1900. In this street were all the services and tradesmen that a country visitor expected to find in the town — banks, hotels, drapers, tobacconists, milliners, grocers, solicitors, auctioneers, chemists and, merchants selling hardware, delph and shoes, and publicans.

Below: Another part of Main Street, c.1912, with that very important new arrival — the motor vehicle. In the door of Thompson's Victoria Temperance Hotel can be seen Miss Eva Thompson, daughter of the proprietor.

This clothes factory, owned by Messrs Stewart and McDonald of Glasgow, was one of several in the town. High class ladies underwear made here was sold in London and other fashionable centres. The manager, a Mr P. Gallagher, is standing in the middle of the group. He later bought the factory from its Scottish owners.

Spectators at the Strabane show, 1911. This was a great social event in the town and was held usually in June. There were butter making competitions, a flower show, competitions for cattle, horses and poultry, and a dog show that was renowned throughout the north west.

Below: McSwiggan's — an appropriately named local public house!

Left: In addition to the main denominations Strabane also had visits from minor religious groups. This gospel caravan was photographed in the outskirts of the town, c.1912.

Below and overleaf: Floods, a frequent hazard in Strabane, were caused by high water in the river Mourne which flowed through the town. The photograph below was taken at the warehouses near the canal. The other photograph, overleaf, was shot on the outskirts. One can see here the smaller houses and cottages which were usually found on the edge of towns.

STRABANE FLOOD—
MOTOR IN DIFFICULTIES.

'The general aspect of Belfast', declared the 1868 edition of *Chambers Encyclopedia*, 'is indicative of life and prosperity, exhibiting all the trade and commerce of Glasgow and Manchester, with far less of their smoke and dirt'. In 1800 the population of Belfast was about 20,000; on the accession of Queen Victoria to the throne it was nearly 70,000 and by the time of her death it had risen to almost 350,000. The photographs in this chapter were taken by an unknown photographer in the early 1870's, when there were about 170,000 inhabitants and the town was in the middle of the hectic social and economic changes which were shaping this important new urban centre.

Well placed at the mouth of Belfast Lough and at the base of the Lagan valley, Belfast at the beginning of the nineteenth century was a prosperous market town and port. Commercial activity expanded rapidly in the town during the following century but the main reason for Belfast's remarkable economic growth was the industrialisation which began in the early 1800's. For this commercial expansion and the development of industries, many of which were dependent on raw materials from abroad, the Belfast port was an extremely important factor and its improvement at various points of the nineteenth century, in particular in the 1860's and 1870's when the Abercorn and Dufferin docks were built, contributed significantly to the town's growth.

The first factories in Belfast manufactured cotton cloth and when the market for cotton declined in the 1820's the factory system was adopted for the manufacture of linen, which had long been an important domestic industry in Ulster. From this time on there was a rapid increase in the number of factories and the production of linen formed the cornerstone of the town's industrialisation. The introduction of the power loom in the factories in the 1850's aided this industrial expansion. Partly to provide the new machinery needed for the factories, an important engineering industry was developed in Belfast. Shipbuilding had been carried on in Belfast prior to the nineteenth century but rapid expansion in this field began only after 1860. Other important industries were ropemaking, food processing and distilling.

The growth of population in Belfast brought tremendous physical charges to the town. For the tens of thousands of people who flocked from the countryside to find work in the factories, vast new areas of industrial housing were constructed. New suburbs were built to house the merchants, industrialists and professional people who left the centre of the town. Sewerage, water, transport and other services were developed during the century. New institutions and commercial buildings were erected. A flourishing school of Belfast architects emerged, creating a new Victorian city out of the old Georgian town.

By the mid 1870's there were various educational institutions as well as literary, scientific and other societies. The Queen's College, opened in 1849, continued to expand its facilities for university education. The Natural History and Philosophical Society, founded in 1820 to promote the investigation of the natural history and antiquities of Ireland, was responsible for the running of a museum, the first in Ireland. Other societies included the People's Literary Institute, the Belfast Medical Society and the Belfast Workingmen's Institute. There were numerous charitable and voluntary bodies. But while these organisations made an important contribution to the life of mid-Victorian Belfast, the town was better known for its business activity.

High Street, as seen here c.1870, was the hub of commercial life in mid-Victorian Belfast. In this street were situated the main offices of merchants, shipbrokers, wholesalers, retailers, insurance agents, vice-consuls and flax agents. There were also several photographers' studios. At the bottom of the street was the Albert Clock, designed by W.J. Barre and completed in 1869. Behind the clock can be seen the side of the customs house and the masts of ships. Off High Street were numerous entries, such as Sugarhouse Entry and Winecellar Entry, where minor tradesmen and labourers lived and where taverns and oyster houses could be found.

Castle Place, c.1870. A continuation of High Street, Castle Place was another important commercial as well as social centre. Three of the largest retail stores in the town were situated here - the Bank Buildings on the left and Robbs on the right, the first and third shops; Anderson and McAuleys, not seen here, was on the extreme left. Fifth on the right was the Ulster Club, a private club for gentlemen, built by Sir Charles Lanyon in 1860. On the opposite side was the Athenaeum Club, founded in 1867 as a more general club with library and newspaper facilities. In the centre of Castle Place, a hackney carriage stand can be observed. The streets were still in a rough state and at intersections or other strategic points there were crossings made of cobble stones or square sets: one can be seen here a short distance before the taxi stand. Proper surfacing of the streets began only in the 1870's, partly as a consequence of the tramway companies being obliged to build squareset surfaces alongside their tracks.

Donegall Place, from the gates of the White Linenhall, looking down to Castle Place, c.1870. The Georgian town houses at the top of Donegall Place, show how much of central Belfast was still residential. The corner of Castle Place, as seen here, was demolished, 1879-81, to replace the old Hercules Street with a new broad Royal Avenue.

Below: A side view of the White Linenhall. Situated in the centre of Belfast, the linenhall, built in 1783-5, reflected the importance of linen in the early growth of Belfast. By 1870 it had long ceased to be used for marketing linen and was utilised for holding civic functions. It also housed the famous Belfast Library and Society for Promoting Knowledge, known as the Linenhall Library, founded in 1788 and still in existence today. The old Linenhall was demolished in the late 1890's and replaced by a new city hall. Belfast became a city officially in 1888.

Upper Arthur Street, at the corner of May Street, c.1870. On the right can be seen the Music Hall, built in 1840 for the Anacreontic Society as a hall for music rehearsals and concerts. By the late 1860's its fortunes had declined and it was being used for general entertainment purposes, as the advertisements show. It later became a church.

# Alex R Hogg

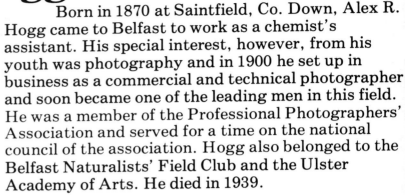

Born in 1870 at Saintfield, Co. Down, Alex R. Hogg came to Belfast to work as a chemist's assistant. His special interest, however, from his youth was photography and in 1900 he set up in business as a commercial and technical photographer and soon became one of the leading men in this field. He was a member of the Professional Photographers' Association and served for a time on the national council of the association. Hogg also belonged to the Belfast Naturalists' Field Club and the Ulster Academy of Arts. He died in 1939.

Transport and industry were 2 of the subjects covered by Hogg in his work. By 1900 the province was amply served by broad gauge railways which connected the main towns, and narrow gauge railways which catered for the remoter areas. Belfast and Derry had their own tramway systems. Horses were still of vital importance for transport: in 1901 around 17,000 horses were used in Ulster for this purpose. The bicycle, especially after the introduction of the safety bicycle in the 1890's, continued to grow in popularity.

The major innovation in transport at the turn of the century was of course the motor vehicle, which first appeared in Belfast around 1895. The growth in number of cars in the early 1900's resulted in acts establishing important regulations for drivers in Ireland. The 1903 motor vehicle act made registration of cars and the carrying of number plates compulsory: it also raised the speed limit from 14 to 20 miles per hour. Another act in 1904 established minimum standards of road worthiness and 6 years later taxes were levied on motor vehicles, with the money being passed to local authorities for road improvements.

Two major figures in transport history with Ulster connections were John Dunlop and Harry Ferguson. The former, who was a Scot, invented the pneumatic tyre in Belfast in 1889, while the latter, from Co. Down, devised the Ferguson tractor which revolutionised world farming.

The industrialisation which occurred mostly in Belfast and the north east provided employment for many of the thousands who left the land, but conditions in this new way of life were often harsh. During the late nineteenth century parliamentary legislation improved working conditions, laying down rules affecting industrial safety and hours of work. However, at the turn of the twentieth century many reforms were still needed. For example, in the linen industry, which was the largest single source of employment, mainly of women and children, conditions were often distinctly unhealthy, due mainly to the processes used, and sometimes made worse by employers' neglect. The atmosphere in the linen mills and factories was usually either very hot and humid, as in most weaving sheds and in the wet spinning room, or filled with dust, as in the roughing, sorting and preparing rooms. Another disturbing aspect of factory life was the employment of children from 12-14 years old, known as half-timers, who worked half the week in the mills and half at school: this system was abolished only in 1920.

At the beginning of the twentieth century the usual total number of hours of work in the linen mills and factories was 55 per week. Women's wages ranged between 9 shillings and 12 shillings per week except for skilled weavers who could earn 18 shillings. To see this in perspective we may note that in 1905 tea cost 2 shillings per lb, bacon, 8-10 pence per lb, eggs, one shilling and 2 pence per dozen. The rent also had to be paid and this was usually about 3 and a half shillings per week. Trade unions were comparatively late in developing in Belfast but in the early 1900's important organisational growth occurred under leaders like James Larkin and William Walker.

Above left and right: Both these vehicles were made by the Chambers motor company, established in Belfast in 1904. The van is a 12 h.p. vehicle, c.1912, while the car is a special touring model, c.1914. Chambers produced high quality vehicles up to 1927 when it was put out of business through competition from Ford and other companies with their mass produced cars.

One of the last horse drawn trams in Belfast, before the conversion of the tramway system to electricity in 1904. First introduced to the town in the early 1870's, the trams were of vital importance for the expansion of Belfast, allowing people to travel considerable distances to their place of work. By 1904 the trams were carrying 23 million passengers a year.

This photograph was taken in 1910, after one of the first air flights in Ireland. The pilot, Harry Ferguson, had constructed the aeroplane from plans in a magazine and he made the first flight in the country at Hillsborough, Co. Down, on 31 December 1909. Ferguson later went on to invent a new type of tractor which transformed farming and made him a multi-millionaire.

Several acts of the late nineteenth century made provisions for the establishment of technical colleges in Ireland. There were a number of institutions in Belfast catering for technical education but they were replaced by the Belfast Municipal College of Technology, which opened in 1907. The college had a wide variety of departments covering subjects such as mechanical engineering, electrical engineering, textiles, commerce, building trades and art. An important part of the college's syllabus was its evening classes for adults. Left: members of the photography class in the college, 1910. Right: lecturer and students of a signwriting class, 1910. Overleaf: a hatmaking class in the college, 1906. This was part of the women's work department which also provided instruction in cookery, dressmaking and laundry work.

These 3 photographs are of workers in a worsted wool factory in Belfast, 1917. As in the linen factories the working day began at 6 am and ended at 6 pm while on Saturday it lasted for only 5 hours.

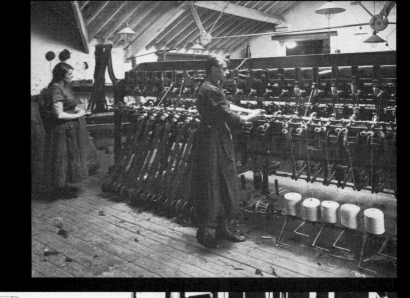

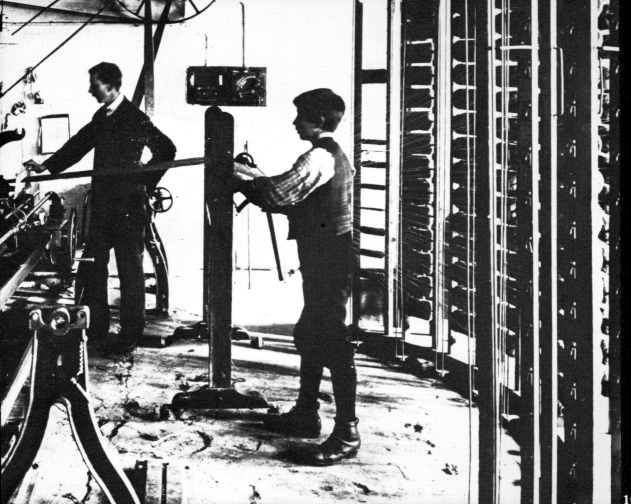

The rapid growth of the population of Belfast in the nineteenth century brought with it tremendous social problems, in particular relating to housing. By the 1850's there was a considerable overcrowding of houses and in a number of areas, squalid slums were to be found, especially among the narrow entries and blind courts which had survived from the beginning of the century and housed the poorest section of the new citizens of Belfast. Several contemporary accounts bear witness to the misery that existed in these areas. Rev. W.M. O'Hanlon, in his *Walks among the poor in Belfast* (Belfast 1853), described vividly the scenes in many of the courts and entries, 'crowded with human beings in the lowest stage of social degradation'. A.G. Malcolm, officer of health for Belfast, published several essays in the 1850's drawing attention to the living conditions in these areas with their overcrowding, inadequate water and sanitary arrangements and connecting them with the epidemics which frequently afflicted the population.

From the 1850's the number of new houses built in the town increased. This was partly a result of the break up of the town property of the Donegall family who owned most of Belfast. The new housing was an improvement on much that had been built before, thanks to a housing by-law of 1848 which imposed certain standards. Houses now had small backyards and piped water, a distinct improvement from the back to back houses with no water, found in the entries. A more important act of 1878 required a back entry, a water closet and ashpit for each house. Efforts were made in the second half of the century to improve the drainage and water supply of Belfast.

The rate of house construction proceeded at an even greater pace after 1878 than before. By 1900 the bulk of the housing in Belfast was of the post 1878 kind and the city compared favourably with other industrial centres in regard to its standard of housing. There were no tenement houses in Belfast and most houses were occupied by one family only, although, with their fairly limited living space these post 1878 dwellings were often overcrowded with the large families which were common.

Little was done to remove or improve the pre-1878 dwellings. There were still many houses with no back access. By the beginning of the twentieth century Belfast was no longer ravaged by the serious diseases of 50 years previous, but typhoid remained a danger especially in areas of bad housing.

In 1906 a government enquiry began in Belfast concerning health conditions in the city. Its report 2 years later urged improvements affecting the water supplies, sewerage, school buildings and conditions of employment. It also drew attention to a number of the older streets, courts and entries which were still inhabited and recommended that they be demolished. The photographs in the chapter were taken in 1911 and are from a small album of 15 photographs of dwellings which were subsequently knocked down, as a result of the enquiry. The identity of the photographer is not known.

Tate's Court, Millfield — a dilapidated survival from eighteenth century Belfast. **109**

Mitchell Street, off Townsend Street, West Belfast, 1911. The whitewashed houses are late eighteenth century dwellings, a remnant from the days when Belfast had been a country market town. This area was demolished around 1914.

Left: Entrance to Mitchell Street. Housing by-laws of 1878 forbade the construction of streets ending in alleyway entrances, as seen here, but such streets built before 1878 were only slowly cleared.

One of the courts, probably Pinkerton's Row, off North Queen Street, West Belfast, 1911. York Street Mill, the largest spinning mill in the world, can be seen dominating the houses as it did the lives of the people in this district.

Left: Dayton Street, 1911. These houses were built probably in the early Victorian period and would have had no water or proper sewerage.

Below: Duffy's Court, near Boundary Street, West Belfast, 1911. Demolition work had already started on this court as part of a redevelopment scheme begun around 1911, following a government report of 1908 which strongly condemned certain districts of old narrow streets and blind courts as insanitary areas, and urged their closure.

# Robert John Welch

The leading photographer in the north of Ireland in the late nineteenth and early twentieth centuries was undoubtedly Robert John Welch (1859-1936). Born at Strabane, Co. Tyrone, he lived for a time in Enniskillen, Co. Fermanagh, where his father ran a photographic business. On the death of his father in 1875 he moved to Belfast and worked for a local photographer, E.T. Church. In 1883 Welch established his own business, and over the next 53 years built up a high reputation as a photographer covering a wide range of fields, including geology, botany, topography, archaeology and ethnography. In his work he dealt with all of Ireland, but especially Ulster: in 1926 he reckoned he had travelled 60,000 miles to photograph antiquities alone. Welch's photographs were used for scientific articles and lectures, as well as for book illustrations, advertisements and publicity purpose. He was official photographer to a number of important industrial firms such as Harland and Wolff and the Belfast Ropeworks Company.

Welch possessed a wide knowledge of many of the subjects he photographed. He was a member of the Royal Irish Academy, the Belfast Naturalist Field Club and the Conchological Society of Great Britain and Ireland: he served as president of the latter 2 societies. To these organisations Welch brought great enthusiasm and learning and he was well known for his generosity and helpfulness. In recognition of his valuable contribution to Irish natural history, Queen's University, Belfast, conferred an honorary M.Sc. on him in 1923.

Of the societies to which Welch belonged, the Belfast Naturalist Field Club was probably his main interest. The club was founded in 1863 to promote interest in natural history and archaeological studies, and to increase knowledge of the geology, botany, zoology and antiquities of the north of Ireland. During the summer it held excursions to different parts of the country while in the winter members read papers at regular meetings: it

# COUNTRYSIDE AND CITY

R.J. Welch, 1903 - in his
famous field club outing hat!

ublished proceedings of the club as well as lists of
ocal species and antiquities, compiled by members.
"he club attracted a wide range of intellectuals.
Besides Welch, at least 4 other of the photographers
n this book were members. F.J. Bigger, the
ntiquarian, and R.L. Praeger, the naturalist, also
elonged to the club.

Over the period from the 1880's to the 1930's
Welch built up a fine collection of negatives of
Belfast street scenes, which provides us today with a
aluable record of the various changes during these
ears. The photographs of Belfast, selected for this
hapter, show the city in the Edwardian era and
nake an interesting comparison with the pictures of
nid-victorian Belfast, seen in an earlier chapter. By
911 the population of the city had arisen to nearly
00,000. Shipbuilding had become the leading
Belfast industry along with linen manufacture.

Members of the Belfast
Naturalists' Field Club at the
Mintiagh lakes in Inishowen on
14 July 1908, during a 3 day visit
of the club to Lough Swilly and
eastern Donegal.

The Ampitheatre, Giant's Causeway, Co. Antrim. Forming an almost exact semi-circle with cliffs 350 feet high, the Ampitheatre was one of the spectacular sights on the 3 miles long Giant's Causeway coast. Consisting of basaltic rock formed be volcanic eruption some 60 million years ago and made in cooling into columns, usually hexagonal in shape, the area was regarded as one of the geological wonders of the world and attracted many visitors. Near the summit of the Ampitheatre, basalt columns, 80 feet high, may be seen, while below them is a broad projection under which are columns 60 feet high. This is a good example of Welch's geological photography.

Launching of the White Star liner, Olympic, 20 October, 1910. For this launching the builders painted the whole vessel white to facilitate the work of 30 photographers, representing the world's press. As official photographer for Harland and Wolff, Welch was responsible for arranging the photographic coverage of the event. The Olympic and its sister ship, the ill-fated Titanic which was still in the dock, each weighed over 45,000 tons and were the largest ships in the world.

Castle Place, Belfast, c.1902. The presence of the trams and the properly surfaced road makes a strong contrast with the photograph of Castle Place in the 1870's, as seen in the chapter on mid-Victorian Belfast. Changes in the emulsion used on plate glass negatives now allowed scenes with crowds to be more easily photographed than three decades earlier.

High Street, Belfast, c.1908.
By 1908 Belfast was the most
populous city in Ireland and the
eighth largest city in the
British Isles. One hundred
years earlier it had been a town
of just over 20,000 inhabitants.

Left: Donegall Place, Belfast,
c.1906. By this time Donegall
Place had ceased to be
residential. On the right is the
grand department store of
Robinson and Cleaver, opened
in the mid 1880's. Busts of
some of the store's most
illustrious customers decorated
the outside of the building,
including Queen Victoria, the
emperor and empress of
Germany and the Maharajah of
Cooch Behar - these can still be
seen today.

# David James Hogg

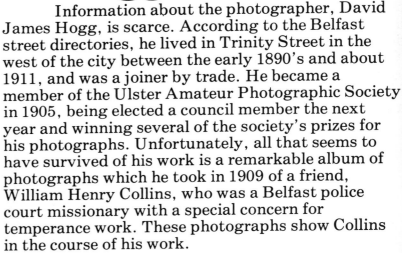

Information about the photographer, David James Hogg, is scarce. According to the Belfast street directories, he lived in Trinity Street in the west of the city between the early 1890's and about 1911, and was a joiner by trade. He became a member of the Ulster Amateur Photographic Society in 1905, being elected a council member the next year and winning several of the society's prizes for his photographs. Unfortunately, all that seems to have survived of his work is a remarkable album of photographs which he took in 1909 of a friend, William Henry Collins, who was a Belfast police court missionary with a special concern for temperance work. These photographs show Collins in the course of his work.

Collins was appointed in 1909 by the temperance committee of the general assembly of the Presbyterian church to act as a police court missionary. He attended the Belfast police court, counselled prisoners in the cells, and in cases where offenders received the benefit of the probation of first offenders act, he was responsible for looking after them. Collins and others like him were the forerunners of our modern probation service: after-care of prisoners at this time was also undertaken by voluntary organisations such as the Prison Gate Mission and the Discharged Prisoners' Aid Society. In addition to this court work, Collins carried his temperance crusade to people's homes, public houses and places of entertainment.

Of the convicted prisoners in Ireland in 1902, 50 per cent were committed for drunkenness or disorderly behaviour while drunk; by 1910 the figure had fallen to slightly under 40 per cent. In Edwardian Belfast, where drink was cheap and pubs were plentiful, there was a high degree of excessive drinking, due partly to the harshness of city and industrial life. Temperance societies took on a new lease of life in the early 1900's and energetically promoted temperance by providing coffee houses and urging tougher licensing laws. Some temperance reformers showed awareness of the social problems

causing drunkenness and advocated various
industrial and housing reforms. An important
development in the temperance movement was the
'Catch-my-pal' total abstinence unions, based on the
idea of each member recruiting a friend. It was
founded in 1909 by an Armagh minister and within
a year had 130,000 pledged members.

A temperance agent!

Left above: Prisoners' cells in the Belfast police court. W.H. Collins, the court missionary is the person in the frock coat on the left. Left: In the police court room. Sir Andrew Newton Brady is the presiding magistrate. The police court, now called the petty sessions, dealt with minor offences, drunkenness and vagrancy. Above right: Young man signing a temperance pledge in the presence of W.H. Collins, some officials of the court and a prison officer. Right: police court surgeon tending to a young charge.

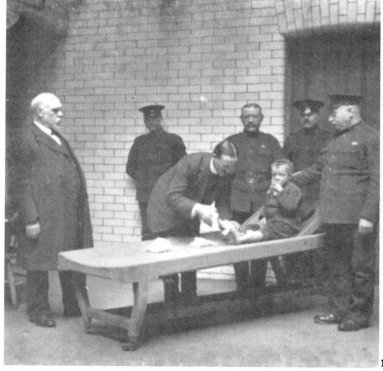

A penny bap and buttermilk were the daily rations for the destitute and prisoners awaiting trial.

Billy, a prison 'trusty' handing in the daily
rations to a prisoner who can be seen inside
the cell, lying on boards.

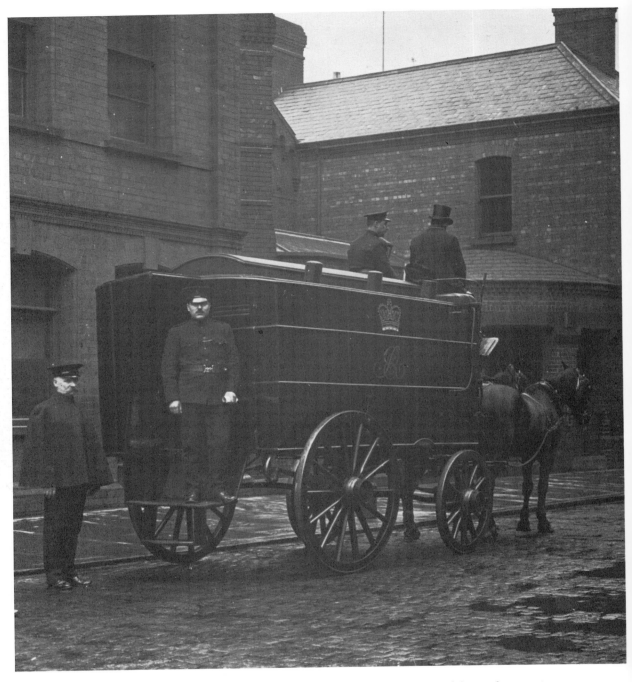

A black maria waiting outside the police court to convey prisoners to and from the court.

Two policemen grooming a horse. In this period the Royal Irish Constabulary in Belfast had a mounted section.

W.H. Collins at work
distributing temperance
literature in a public house,
Shankill Road.

W.H. Collins in Joseph McKibbin's billiard hall, Shankill Road. Billiards, football and dog racing were the most popular sports among the working classes in Belfast at this time.

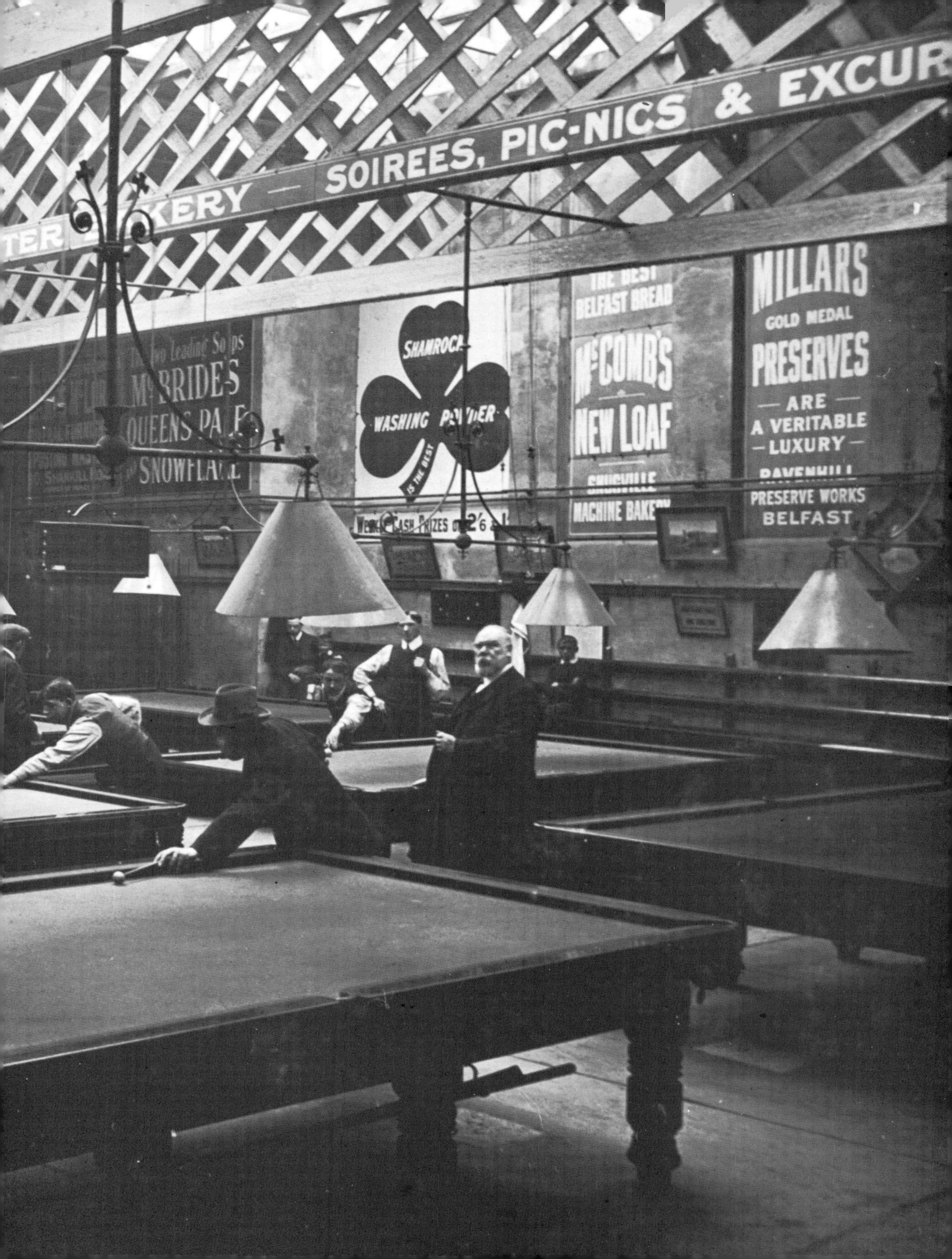
SOIREES, PIC-NICS & EXCUR
SHAMROCK
WASHING POWDER
IS THE BEST
THE BEST BELFAST BREAD
McCOMB'S
NEW LOAF
MACHINE BAKERY
MILLARS
GOLD MEDAL
PRESERVES
ARE
A VERITABLE
LUXURY
PRESERVE WORKS
BELFAST
SNOWFLAKE

# Acknowledgements

I would like to thank the many people who have helped me write *Shadows on Glass*. My work was greatly aided by the kind assistance of the staffs of the Linenhall Library, the Public Record Office of Northern Ireland, the Ulster Folk Museum, the Ulster Museum, Queen's University Library and the Belfast Central Library. For their generous help I am especially indebted to Mr Bill Crawford, Mrs Phyllis McAtackney, Mr Michael McCaughan, Miss Emara MacNeill, Mrs Wendy Osborne, Mr James Vitty, Mr Patrick Roche and Miss Vicki Moltke.

Very useful information, in their respective fields of study, was given to me by Mrs Elizabeth Malcolm, Mr Gerry Cleary, Mrs Emily Boyle and Mr Hugh Dixon. Dr William Vaughan kindly allowed me to call on his great knowledge of the nineteenth century Irish countryside. Professors E.R.R. Green, J.C. Beckett, E.E.Evans, and David Miller, at the Institute of Irish Studies, gave me extremely valuable advice on many occasions. I am grateful as always to Professor T.W. Moody for his encouragement and advice. To Dr Joe Dundee and Mrs Isobel Crozier, my thanks are due for their kind hospitality and information.

Mr William Lyttle and Miss Gail Pollock provided me with many first class photographic prints, for which I am grateful. Miss Pat Smyth kindly did most of the typing. My father was of great help in the proof reading and often made very useful suggestions. Finally thanks are due to the Traditional Arts Committee of the Northern Ireland Arts Council for their interest and support.

For permission to reproduce photographs, acknowledgements are gratefully made to the following: the Public Record Office of Northern Ireland for the Young photographs; Dr Joe Dundee for the McKinney photographs; the trustees of the Ulster Folk and Transport Museum for the Green photographs; Mr C.T. Rutledge and Miss Pat Lithgow for the Hutton photographs; Mr Peter Verschoyle for the Shaw photographs; Miss Joyce Holden for the Holden photographs; Mr H.D.H. Cooper for the Cooper photographs; Miss Mabel Colhoun for the Glass photographs; the Linenhall Library for the D.J. Hogg and mid-Victorian Belfast photographs; the trustees of the Belfast Museum for 3 of the Welch photographs and Dr Joe Dundee, Mrs Isobel Crozier and Mr G.M. Stelfox for each of the 3 other Welch photographs; the Department of the Environment for the Belfast slum photographs; the Belfast College of Technology, Thompson Reid Ltd., Mrs Hugh Crymble, Town Clerk, Belfast, for the A.R. Hogg photographs.

# Bibliography

Many books and parliamentary papers were consulted in the writing of this book but the following were especially important:

J.C. Beckett and R.E. Glasscock. *Belfast: origin and growth of an industrial city*. London, 1967.
*Belfast Telegraph*. 1 September 1970. This centenary edition contains several relevant articles.
L.M. Cullen. *Six generations*. Cork, 1970. *Townlife*. Dublin, 1973.
E.E. Evans. *Irish folk ways*. London, 1957. 4th impression, 1967.
W.J. Fitzpatrick. *Sailing ships of Mourne*. Newcastle, 1967.
Basil Greenhill. *The merchant sailing ship : a photographic history*. Newtown Abbot, 1970.
Lord George Hill. *Facts from Gweedore*. London, 5th edition, 1887: reprint, Belfast, 1971, with introduction by E.E. Evans.
Emrys Jones. *A social geography of Belfast*. London, 1960.
S. McCullough. *Ballynahinch: centre of Down*. Belfast, 1968.
Noel Nesbitt. *Changing face of Belfast*. Belfast, 1968.
K.B. Nowlan. *Travel and transport in Ireland*. Dublin, 1973.
*The agricultural output of Northern Ireland, 1925 . . . with a survey of the agricultural statistics of Northern Ireland from 1847 to 1927*. Belfast, HMSO, c.87, 1928.
T.W. Moody and J.C. Beckett (ed.) *Ulster since 1800*. 2 series: (1) *A political and economic survey*; (2) *A social survey*. London, 1955, 1957.
Jeffrey Simpson. *The way life was: a photographic treasury from the American past*. New York, 1974. This book inspired the method of presentation of photographs in *Shadows on Glass*.
Obituary notices on R.J. Welch in *The Irish Naturalists' Journal*. Vol. vi, no.6 (Nov. 1936).
H.E. Wilson. Rise and decline of the iron ore and bauxite industry of Co. Antrim. *Proceedings of Belfast Natural History and Philosophical Society*. Second series. Vol. 7 (1965), pp14-23.